For all the
wonderful people
who ARE,
Rose Valley.
Capt. Dean Nichols

Summer 2015

The Highline Trail

The
Highline
Trail

Dean Nichols

RESOURCE *Publications* · Eugene, Oregon

Resource Publications
A division of Wipf and Stock Publishers
199 W 8th Ave, Suite 3
Eugene, OR 97401

The Highline Trail
By Nichols, Dean
Copyright©2011 by Nichols, Dean
ISBN 13: 978-1-61097-438-7
Publication date 4/11/2011

Contents

Acknowledgments

Who would have dreamed, fifty-five years ago, that that 52 lb. little boy, who jauntily carried his ten pound pack, without complaint, all the way on the seven day trek around a volcanic peak, in the wilds of the mountains of Southwestern Washington State, would once again be teamed with the author - this time to bring the story of our adventure to life.

All that I, the Author, did was walk those silent trails, hearing that awesome wilderness speak to my heart and hand, to write the simple story of our passing.

But this caring, and able "Production Engineer", gave the world, in this book, that "simple story" in a form that makes it live again in the hearts and minds of any explorer into the wonder that is the human spirit.

Thank you, Denny Hill.

For Alma,

and for Lloyd,

and for Sherry,

who have gone home

before us.

Sherry and Alma

"His foundation is in
the holy mountains."
  Ps. 87:1

"...the mountains and the hills
shall break forth before you
into singing,..."
  Is. 55:12

"...Thus saith the Lord God
to the mountains,
and to the hills..."
  Ezek. 36:4

"Where there is no vision,
the people perish..."
  Pr. 29:18

[My beloved son, Lloyd, and I had taken our boat on a two weeks' hunting trip across Alaska's Lake Louise, Lake Susitna, Lake Tyone, and north down the Tyone River.

Twice, we passed the empty village of Tyone, and each time there was much more than just the intense awareness of an abandoned village, there was much, much more. This poem tries to grasp what it was.]

The Mountain's Call

Wrapped in the mystery of a people gone
and held in the spell of a spirit,
that is all that is left to tell of their flight,
save a few tumbling cabins
and the empty shell of a crude boat,
I listen for the voice of the past;
and I hear,
faintly, but clearly, and with a power indescribable
and echoing down the long, cold waters
of Lake Tyone,
I hear the mountain's call.

Are they there,
frozen forever in the ageless ice of the mountains,
these people of the Village of Tyone?
Are they calling to my searching,
questioning mind
from their icy grave
and saying,
"Come, share with us the mountain's
bewitching beauty
(and the mountain's terror)
and we will tell you our story."?

Where have they gone,
these people of the Village of Tyone?
Did they,
one day in the measureless past,
fail to resist, as I can barely resist,
the enveloping magnetism
of the mountain's call?

May 25, 1962
(From the book, ISLANDS OF EXPERIENCE, by the same author.)

Prologue

The preceding poem was brought to life, in Alaska, and many, many years after this simple story was written. But it makes a poignant point: There is a "presence" emanating from a mountain; especially, a volcanic peak, even if dormant.

There are apologists for science who insist that Mt. Sinai was just an active volcano. Ah, but from there came the Ten Commandments, the fundamental basis of all, world law. And when Moses came down from that mountain, his face was shining so brightly, the people could not look upon it.

If, as the Good Book also speaks, "...even the rocks will cry out...," can one say, that a mountain cannot speak?

Mountain peaks, especially, are often shrouded in a mantle of cloud; their sides shrouded in a mantle of snow. But to the observant, listening heart, they are also shrouded in a mantle of mystery, a mantle of Spirit. And that Spirit speaks, and flows, and calls.

The Cascade Range is pierced by a surprising number of volcanic peaks, all dormant, the geologists say; although smaller, relatively unimpressive Mt. St. Helens, commanded the world's attention, just a few years ago, by blowing her top.

Twenty-five miles or so south of our home, in White Salmon, Washington, and across the Columbia River, Mt. Hood was our daily view. Eighty miles or so north, one of the most beautiful mountain peaks in the world, Mt. Rainier "broods" over Seattle, Tacoma, and Puget Sound. Twenty-five to thirty miles northwest, Mt. St. Helens still trembles with uncertainty. But thirty miles due north, "Our" Mountain, 12,307 foot, Mt. Adams, waits, and calls, and sends out her silent, inviting song.

According to U.S. Forest Service maps; there was an "Around the mountain trail." And, the Forest Service people assured us, dangerously, we were to find, "Oh yes, there is a good trail, all the way around the mountain." Ah, but the irrepressible optimism of the human spirit. This story chronicles the results of that optimism, optimism held by two pairs of very ordinary parents, and by seven, very ordinary, but vibrantly alive, young children.

The story begins slowly, even with, admittedly, an undramatic, "Annual Christmas Letter" tone. It is a homely story, written in a simple, uncomplicated style, if, indeed, there is any style.

For it wasn't until we were well out on the trail, that that Spirit of the Mountain began to really stir the soul of this young, unpolished author, that here, now, indeed, was a dramatic, family adventure unfolding. So stay with this simple story, and travel the Highline Trail with us.

Dean Nichols
September, 1990

Chapter I

A Single Step

White Salmon, Washington, Summer, 1955: It has been written, "Without dreams, even unfulfilled dreams, we should die." Our family was very much alive. And so it was really not unexpected that the dream of walking the nearly sixty mile, "Round the mountain trail," should begin taking the form of a vision.

Still, we "older, and thus wiser," parents shared in the chatter, knowing, in our "wisdom," that the idea would remain just a dream.

But we did not reckon with that irrepressible enthusiasm, that unquenchable optimism, of our 14 year old son, Lloyd. He had inherited from his Grandfather, (his Mother's Father,) a large measure of that oneness with the wilderness, more characteristic of the great frontiersmen of the early West. He "knew" we could do it.

The months passed, and he kept reminding us of our own teachings that, "Families should do as many things together as they can," and, "You only have your kids once." I think the thing that finally changed talk to action was when he said, rather disgustedly, "Well, we probably couldn't make it anyway, ' cause you and Mommie are too old. "

Well, as the Chinese say, "Even the longest journey begins with but a single step;" and so we took that first step by studying catalogs for pack boards, sleeping bags, and camping gear, seeking information on trails, and on various types of rations, making lists of gear that must, or should go, and of course, studying all available maps. For a long time we designed our study along the idea of carrying all of our supplies on our backs. But as "Bugs" and Lorraine Hill, and their children, Sherry, age 12, and Denny, age 9, became interested, they convinced us of the wisdom of taking our two horses, both to make our packs lighter, but also as emergency transportation in the event of illness or injury. And besides, Lorraine was afraid we couldn't carry enough food on our backs to keep her from getting hungry. As it turned out, by taking the horses we were able to take extra clothing, extra food rations, and the two-burner, gas stove, which greatly eased meal preparations for our excellent cooks and good sports, Lorraine and Alma.

In November of 1955 our hopes and plans took their first, almost fatal blow. The reckless action on the part of a young soldier involved Alma and me in an auto collision that demolished our car, and put us both in the hospital; I with an injured knee, and crushed foot, and Alma with an injured back, and shattered pelvis. Lying for eight weeks flat on her back certainly made her wonder if she would ever walk again, before even considering carrying a pack over fifty-five miles of wilderness trail around a Mountain. And the fact of these injuries further added strength to the skeptics' voiced beliefs that we just couldn't make it, that it was foolhardy to attempt such a trip with children, even if all were in excellent physical condition. And there were times when we, ourselves wondered if perhaps they were not right. We never were sure whether we were proving to our Doctor how tough we were in spite of the wreck, or how good a bone welder he was.

However, early in February of '56, we drove out to the Mt. Adams District Ranger Station, in the deep snow, and discussed the trip with the Forest Service. Even though there were, at the time, twelve foot high banks of snow on both sides of the road, and we wondered how it could all possibly melt in time, we were much encouraged to make the trip. And we were told that the "Round the mountain trail" was in excellent condition: This, we were later to find, was a dangerous exaggeration. Although that danger, mostly the lack of trail markings, put an extra zest in the adventure, the danger was very real.

Our studies showed that in order to cross the Big Muddy River we would have to penetrate the Yakima Indian Reservation from Goat Butte to the Big Muddy Bridge, far down on the east side of the Mountain; and this would require a permit approved by the Tribal Council of the Yakima Indians.

So on the 26th of February we sent our first letter to the Yakima Indian Agency, requesting permission to "cross over the bridge." Three letters and five months later, we received with excitement the little, pink slip granting the permission so vital to the realization of-our vision. Thinking of bears, cougars, and wolves, we had some serious concerns, as we read in the fine print that no fire arms would be allowed. Later, however, Bugs was successful, while in Yakima, in obtaining limited permission to carry side arms.

Friday, August 3rd. The last week before our trek was to begin. Every evening for Bugs and me, and every day for Lorraine and Alma, was a "madhouse," with last minute preparations. On Monday evening I flew a Piper Cub out, and looked over the possibilities of a shortcut between Cougar Guard Station and Shadow Lake, and believed that I found a passage. This was the only part of the journey that had really troubled me, as I studied the maps. The trail, as shown on the maps, made a considerable detour, in that area, and I felt that, if we could successfully make the shortcut, we could make the last leg of the long walk, between Cougar Guard Station, via Shadow Lake; to our timberline camp and the cars, in one day.

Having by now firmly decided that the horses were a part of the adventure, we again nearly gave up all hopes when on Tuesday, a stray, stud horse broke into our pasture, and beat our two horses to ribbons. But in the next two days, after treatment and penicillin shots, the veterinarian told us that, although "Chico" couldn't go, we could use our "Paint," "Benny." And we found that we could borrow a big beauty, named "Red," that I used to own. Although we felt sorry for Benny, with all his cuts and bruises, we laughed at the prospect of color slides with that beautiful, red-brown and white horse all splotched with brilliant, purple, disinfectant spray.

Saturday, August 4th. We were up early and started final assembly of supplies and the loading of packs. We brought Red to the house and practiced loading him with his pack. This was the first such experience for the horse, as well as for us. The total food for our family filled one, Army duffel bag, and weighed eighty pounds. The women had packed the entire needs for each meal in individual bags, and then placed the bags in the duffel bag in their proper order. Each bag was marked for the meal, and the day. We could thus predetermine exactly how much food to take. The rest of our gear, canvasses, sleeping bags, extra blankets, cooking utensils, gas stove, cameras, and other gear, plus the food, totaled approximately two hundred seventy-five pounds for our family. We loaded two hundred pounds on Red, and the balance in our packs. We had to completely repack Red three times, but we finally found an arrangement that seemed most secure.

Arranging our personal packs became an interesting problem, since the weight that each could comfortably carry without giving out at a critical time was in itself, critical. After a previous weekend, overnight "test hop" of two miles each way, Alma felt that her healing back would stand ten pounds for quite a spell, and in our arranging at home, we found that the cooking utensils came to just that. I took the two-burner gas stove, and six extra one-quart cans of gas, (A single, two-gallon can would have sloshed around too much.) for a pack of about twenty-five pounds. Judy, age 15, and Lloyd and Rod, each age 14, didn't complain at about twelve pounds each, and little Jo Ann, age 12, did well with just the axe and shovel and spare coat, for a total of about ten pounds.

The Hills, apparently, didn't feel that they could leave as much civilization behind as we, for Bugs, and Lorraine's younger brother, Bobbie Pierson, age 17, came up with forty pound packs each, Lorraine a twenty-five pound pack, and even 12 year old Sherry, and nine year old Denny, ten pound packs each. Still, I must admit, I personally, surely appreciated that big plastic bag full of fresh celery and carrot sticks in Lorraine's pack.

Sunday, August 5th. 10:00 AM. Bugs, Bobbie, who was also Judy's boyfriend, Denny, Lloyd, and I left home with the Jeep Station Wagon and towing the trailer with the two horses aboard. I should say here that if there are some hopes for romance in this story because of the above statement, "Judy's boyfriend," I'm afraid I must dash them now. For remember that, not only were there four, adult chaperones in the party, but also five eager, little tattletales in the form of younger brothers and sisters. Even so, both Judy and Bobbie, as well as all the rest, were already eagerly looking forward to a similar challenge the next summer.

As we pulled up through the Trout Lake Valley, we were thrilled with the majesty of "Our Mountain" with those beautiful, billowing, white clouds boiling around it. "Beautiful, billowing, white clouds." As we stopped at Morrison Creek Camp to check the horses, it started to rain, and the closer we drew to timberline, the harder it rained. When we finally stopped at the timberline camp above Cold Spring Camp, we were greeted with torrents of hail and rain, flashes of lightning, and peels of thunder. We huddled in the car until the storm passed, then built a fire, and saddled up the horses.

1:25 PM. Bugs and I rode out to check the first leg of the trail. We found it in very poor condition, and we had to circle around every so often, just to find the trail again.

3:00 PM. We started back from the Morrison Creek Trail junction without finding where the trail led from there on, and arrived back at timberline camp an hour later. Lorraine, Sherry, and Alma, and the rest of our family, Judy, Rodney, and Jo Ann, plus Hill's male dog "Jinks," a purebred something, and our two, female, purebred nothings, "Margy" and "Itch" had arrived, a thirty member party of Mazamas had come down off the Mountain, and the clouds had started really breaking up.

All started looking well again until I noticed how Bobbie was holding his hand, and Alma her stomach. Bobby had poured gasoline on the fire, and had seriously burned three fingers. Alma had developed severe stomach cramps, and I finally had to make up her bed in the back of the station wagon, and put her to bed. About 7:00, the cramps were so severe, Lloyd and I decided to take her to the Doctor. So down the mountain we drove, with Alma in bed on an air mattress, holding her tummy. But as we reached Cold Spring Camp, the cramps suddenly left completely. We stopped and debated what to do. But Alma thought we ought to drive on down into the village of Trout Lake, since we were that far, not so much to make sure that she was all right, but to get cigarettes for Bobbie, who had nearly driven her crazy earlier with his nervous fidgets. The only smoker in the group, he had, of all times, chosen this trip as an opportunity to quit smoking, and had, of course, brought no cigarettes along. It wasn't that she meant at all to encourage smoking, but she just felt there would be enough problems on the long trek, without having to nurse a "nervous norvous" with nicotine fits.

As we drove back up the Mountain, a huge bear ran up the road ahead of us, and a little later a coyote flashed across our headlights. When we arrived back at timberline, we found a group of anxious people more happy that we had returned, than interested, or frightened at our account of the wild animals.

It had grown quite late by this time, so, with a suspicious eye on the passing storm clouds, but with determination to at least begin our journey, in spite of the weather and our two casualties, we went to bed.

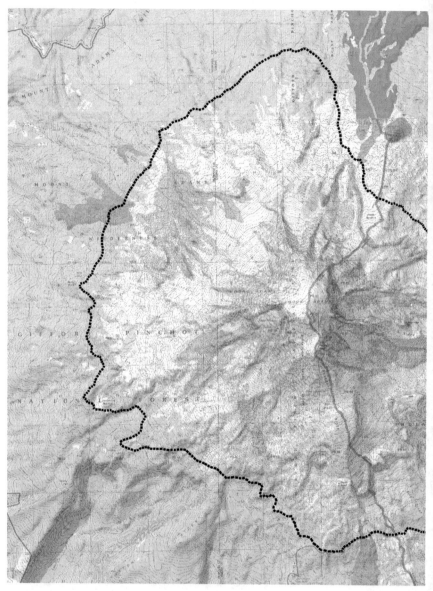

Topographical map of Mt. Adams area

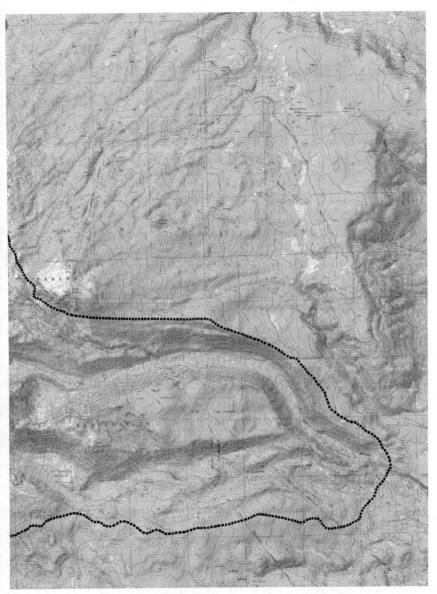

(dark line represents approximate trail route)

Will You Listen?

Will you listen to my song
    if I sing to you?
I'm not a robin, spreading the forest with notes
tumbling all over each other;
I'm not a thrush, whose long song
fills the spaces as completely
as the breeze fills the spaces
between the evergreen boughs;
nor am I that breeze brushing the trees
and singing the soft and soothing song
that breezes sing.

I am but a man;
and my song is words.
And though intelligence and denotation
are the burden of words,
sometimes, instead, I'd have them sing
and spread their message like a robin's song,
challenging your mind to put together
the fascinating puzzle
that is clearly there.

Sometimes I'd have them sing
as the thrush would sing,
filling the spaces
so that you feel complete,
knowing that the message feeds your heart
even though the mind cares not to comprehend.

And then sometimes
I'd have them sing as the breezes sing,
no notes, no messages,   .
but only soft and soothing sounds
that reach into the soul
and do not tell at all,
but rather, leave that quiet, deep awareness:
all is well.

But I must sing
as surely as the birds must sing
or breeze must blow.
I must sing.
Will you listen?

July-September, 1971
(From the book, A POET'S SKETCH, by the same author)

Chapter II

Trail Dust On Our Feet

Monday, August 6th, 1956. 5:00 AM. We were awakened at dawn by giggling kids. It seems as though that was the last thing we heard last night too. I was wondering if this giggling would wear out as the kids wore down, or would it be the same thing every night and morning.

Last night's storm had disappeared, and I was anxious to get every one out of bed, and moving out upon the trail. We found the fastest method of getting the women out of bed was to let the air out of the air mattresses, so Alma and Lorraine were soon up. But we quickly learned that we had to make, and enforce, several laws among the seven kids; and one of them was, absolutely not to let air out of each other's air mattresses until time to get up in the morning.

We soon had our delightful breakfast, and while Lorraine and Alma cleaned up the dishes and camp, we had the kids each rolling their own bed rolls and helping Bugs and me pack the horses, Benny and Red. Bugs had to repack Benny twice before we felt the pack was comfortable and secure. This was a new experience for Bugs and Benny as well as for Red and me.

10:30 AM. All packed and ready to start for Looking Glass Lake, our intended destination for the day. Alma's stomach, though still a little touchy, was not giving her any real trouble; and Bugs had done such a fine job of dressing Bobbie's burns that we felt it not an unreasonable risk to reach out a day or two from the cars and see how things went. So we took our first pictures, in weather warm and clear, and started down the trail.

We had very little trouble with the trail as far as the Morrison Creek Trail junction. There were only a few rest stops and readjustments of packs. We stopped here at noon for our lunch, and to rest the horses. We unpacked and unsaddled them, and staked them out in the meadow. That seemed, at first a bit of extra work. But we had brought no extra food for the horses, so we felt that every moment to graze would be needed by them. By the time we finished the long walk, we were certain that that had been a wise decision. And anyway, the repeated unpacking, and repacking developed our skills so, that it became but minutes to accomplish.

There was great good humor, as we ate our lunch, but we laughed, and wondered how long it would be funny, since every lunch was prepacked, and the same, and consisted of sardines, rye bread, cheese, raisins, and a candy bar apiece. Rodney didn't like sardines at all, and had very little respect for cheese, so he did a little trading for more raisins. One of the other laws we adults had decreed was, no mooching off the other family unless they had eaten all they wanted. For some reason, I was constantly being accused by the kids of breaking this rule. As soon as our lunch was finished, someone would dig a hole in which to bury all our papers and tin cans. By the time we unsaddled the horses, ate lunch, cleaned up and repacked the horses, an hour was gone.

While Bugs and I and the boys were reloading the horses, Alma and Lorraine had done some scouting for the trail, and had found a very good one leading, as we thought it

should, straight toward Crofton Ridge. Although the trail was new to us from here, it was again, easy to follow. Oh, that "well maintained" trail gave us many logs to detour around, and there were many snow banks to cross over; but as we stepped out upon the trail again, after our lunch, we were all excited by the opening scenery. The trees were not crowded in on us; and there were many, small, but refreshing, clear streams.

We were all keeping an eye on Crofton Ridge, wondering just where we would cross it, as it was the major climb for the day.

With such beautiful, mountain summer weather, and with the thrill of adventure lifting our spirits, it was hard for us to resist using all of our camera film. Every bend in the trail challenged us with a new and stirring view. Sleeping Beauty looked not at all like the Indian Princess, sleeping on her back, as seen from Trout Lake Valley. And she appeared to be just a "stone's throw away" from us, and to our left; and, reaching high to our right, impressing the presence of the Mountain upon us, was massive, Avalanche Glacier.

2:00 PM. We had reached the top of Crofton Ridge, the side of which had been so steep that the trail zigzagged several times before reaching the top. This had been a real climb, and had taken some of the zest out of the kids. The wisecracks were not as frequent, because climbing and laughing at the same time, at that altitude, just did not mix.

The look back down from Crofton Ridge was like looking into another world. The little streams wound down among the Pine trees, and through the grassy meadows, as far as we could see; yet looking ahead of us we saw yet a different world. It looked like Avalanche Glacier had washed a million tons of rocks down from the side of the Mountain. And possibly, that is not an exaggeration.

Our next mile was difficult travel, picking our way across that rocky wash, for there was absolutely no sign of a trail left. And we crossed our first, major, mountain stream. But the horses behaved like regular, old pack mules, and crossed the stream with no trouble at all. Itch, however, one of our own, two dogs, a tiny Fox Terrier, fell into the flood, and Alma had to fish her out.

We were all concerned about poor, little Itch. She had been dumped off at our home two weeks before our trip. But to add a real problem, one week before we left, she had to have a rush operation, or I'm afraid all of the male wolves and coyotes on Mt. Adams would have been following us. She still had stitches in her tummy, and the family was constantly worrying about her "incision." But the coming days were to prove that she was as tough as any in the troupe.

The rocks and boulders that had been washed down were strikingly colorful. Nearly every vivid color of the spectrum was laid out before us; and we couldn't resist taking color pictures of them. Out in the middle of that incredible, rock wash, we crossed Salt Creek, and yes, it tasted salty. The horses loved it, and crystals had formed on the small, evergreen trees near its edge, giving them a frosted appearance.

We were soon into the timber again, and lost sight of "our" Mountain. Every one had gotten noisy again, as it was down hill, and the trail was quite good. Suddenly, we were stopped by a repeated, piercing, shrill whistle. The sound, unfamiliar to any of us, had some suspecting it was a cougar screaming. But we had come into a colony of Whistling Marmots, harmless, little, prairie dog like animals, living in a steep rock slide. They would sit up straight on a rock, without a motion until you'd swear that they weren't real; then suddenly they would whistle that single note of incredibly loud, shrill, piercing sound and disappear out of sight. All three dogs, of course, tried to catch them, but as a dog would close in on one, it would vanish, and another would appear a dozen or so yards away. They very soon had some bewildered dogs completely exhausted.

3:00 PM. We sighted Looking Glass Lake, where we were scheduled to spend the night, and fish for trout, which were clearly plentiful. But after the walk, down off the main trail to the lake, we decided to let the mosquitoes keep the place, and to continue on up the trail in hopes of finding Lake Camp, as shown on one of our maps to be a half mile or so from the lake.

But after a mile of strenuous hiking produced no Lake Camp, some wanted to stop at the first, reasonably likely spot. But we persuaded the tired and sore packers to keep going. And in another half mile we finally came to the most beautiful meadow, full of deliciously, tasty grass, according to the horses; and a look around discovered a very fine camp site. We all fell in love with it. Magnificent Mt. Adams stood high and mighty guard over the far end of the meadow. After making very sure that all wanted to stay, I showed them the sign I had found leaning against a tree, "Graveyard Camp," not Lake Camp, as shown on our map. We even found the grave. But not one of this weary team wanted to move on.

This was Monday night; and the menu called for "Pronto Pups." For some reason, Bugs, instead of Lorraine, got the job for their family of mixing up the batter to go around the wieners. Alma and Bugs immediately got into an argument as to whether the dough should be thick or thin. So they both ignored their advisor, Judy, who was the only one who had ever made them before, and Bugs made a thick batter, and Alma made a pasty dough. What a doughy time they had, there by the camp fire, getting those things into foil and into the coals. Both cooks, of course, were insistent on keeping their own separate from the other's, as they just "knew" the other fellow's wouldn't be any good.

I was quite dubious about the whole mess, especially when I found out that neither Bugs, Lorraine, nor Alma

31

had ever made them before. But much to everyone's pleasant surprise, they turned out to be delicious. And Bugs couldn't tell his from Alma's. To go with them, we had powdered milk and ovaltine, carrot and celery sticks, and instant, vanilla pudding. And as the last crumbs were cleaned up, and everyone felt comfortably stuffed, we appreciated the accuracy of planning by our rations "experts."

Pronto Pups: I think the aura of home was still shielding us from the presence of the Mountain. Had we been eating raw meat, and herbs dug from the ground, the fact, of our wilderness position would have washed that aura away. But like the Holy Spirit, the Spirit of the Mountain is not rude. He will not force Himself upon us. We were not to eat raw meat and herbs, but the coming days were to wash that aura away. The Mountain was there.

Bugs had borrowed two Mountain Tents, for himself and Lorraine, and for Denny and Sherry; but Denny and Sherry felt cheated if they couldn't sleep out under the stars, with the rest of the kids, with just tarpaulins spread over their sleeping bags. So Alma and I quickly agreed to trade places with them. Although we did have more "privacy," and the tents provided a "Dressing room," it became no small chore, developing the comical art of crawling carefully through the small tube on each end of the tent, and dressing and undressing on our knees, with our shoulders and head brushing the top and walls at the same time.

Bugs assumed the task every night, of pitching both tents; and to save half of one set of stakes, he tied the sides of the two tents together. Anyone who has ever slept on plastic air mattresses will agree that, although they are very comfortable, they squeak terribly every time one rolls over. Although we were in separate "rooms," we soon found ourselves calling to the Hills, and they to us, to settle down, so we could get some sleep. Also, the two tents being tied together became an advantage, or, disadvantage. If one family thought the other was sleeping too late in the morning, we could jerk on the tabs inside our tent, opposite the ropes, and could make the other tent appear to be coming down on top of them. We called it our "Inter-tent Communication System."

As we prepared for bed, the excitement of sleeping out really stirred the kids' blood; a moaning wind came sneaking down from the Mountain; and that sign, "Graveyard Camp," seemed to glare at us. Kids camping out always seem to be inspired to tell the most blood curdling yarns, and I'll admit here, we were all a little afraid of the dark. I was about to call to them to hush and go to sleep, till Alma reminded me that when we were kids, we too were stirred by that irrepressible thrill of sleeping under the stars. The last I remembered, after the ghost stories, was kids telling each other they hoped they didn't have to get up in the middle of the night.

Painting

You take the brush
and place the oils on canvas there
      and let me play with words.

Paint mountains high, you dare;
but is it really fair
to thrust the brush into my hand?
My medium is words, and rather
with my pen I'd paint the frozen land
and stack the granite crags
into the sky.

Late in the afternoon I'll brush
the shadows deep in those ravines
and glint the softened amber glow
from off the ridges torn
with blowing snow.

And lower down I'll turn
the green trees blue and maybe catch
the sparkle of a waterfall;
or is it ice just standing tall
and waiting for the warmth of spring
to flow again down to the sea?

I took the brush
and daubed the canvas bare
and felt a faint, creative spark,
I must admit;
but would you really care
if here instead on this plain page
I place the symbols man calls words
in such a pattern
that the mountains rise before your eyes,
and laugh once more with sunlight
before they drift into the night and die?

I'll try again;
but really, I believe my pen
is better fitted to my hand.

January 24, 1971
(From the book, ISLANDS OF EXPERIENCE, by the same author)

Chapter III

Memories Are Made Of This

Tuesday, August 7th, 1956. 5:45 AM. Alma's and my air mattresses having gone flat, and the horses stomping around, because they were out of grass, I got up and moved them, built a fire, then hurried out with a shovel to beat the morning rush. It soon became a standing joke, knowing that everyone had difficulty finding a spot with a reasonable amount of privacy, and yet with a picture window view.

Last night the only thing we found wrong with our camp was the quarter mile hike back up the trail for water. In my little aforementioned trip, I discovered a fine spring not over a hundred feet from camp.

6:15 AM. With hotcakes "sizzling in the pan," and with the aroma of boiling coffee drifting through the camp, the sun came beaming over the south side of the Mountain. Wild flowers had been adding profuse color to our whole travel time, but I believe they were especially beautiful this morning. The aches and pains of last evening were largely gone, and all were eager to head up the trail.

9:30 AM. With packs all loaded, the camp clean, and the fire dead, we moved out upon the trail. In ten minutes we came to a junction and swung north on a section of the Cascade Crest Trail. This trail, which reaches from Canada to Mexico, was so well maintained and easy to follow, that I guess it was too much temptation to the

boys, who, by noon, had gotten themselves seriously "in the doghouse" for ranging out of sight and sound with film and first aid supplies.

Spectacular pictures of Mt. St. Helens to the west, and Mt. Rainier to the north, and, of course, the always new and terrible grandeur of our own Mt. Adams, frequently broke into view, even though most of the time we were traveling in heavy timber. But every time, our hearts were stirred, deeply, by that glorious ambivalent *message* that emanated from those mountains. At once, they spoke a magnetic call, and, a warning. This was not, I think, unlike the voice of God: "Come close to me, obey my laws, and I will give you glory. Violate, or worse, dismiss my laws, and reap the fury of my justice."

The snow patches were growing larger and more frequent; and we often had to detour around the steep ones with the horses, or make hazardous, zigzag crossings down the faces of them.

11:45 AM. A beautiful spot for lunch, so we stopped, unloaded the horses, and staked them out to graze. As we unloaded the packs, we noticed our fingers getting sore from the frequent pulling of ropes. Sherry and Jo Ann went down to the far end of the shallow, snow melt lake, where the water had risen over the soft green grass, and went swimming. Others of us sat on a log with our bare feet in the cool, refreshing water as we ate. Resourceful Alma temporarily repaired Judy's shoe with nylon fish line; and we all carried on our first real battle with mosquitoes. For all the mosquitoes though, we all laughed at Benny, straddling a small tree, scratching them off his belly.

1:00 PM. After reloading our tummies, reloading our cameras, and reloading our horses, we started on. There were many deer tracks in the trail, and there was occasional bear sign, but we have seen no wild animals so far, except more Whistling Marmots. A check against the mileposts along the Crest Trail showed that we were "racing along" at about two miles per hour. Noname, Riley, and Mutton creeks came in swift succession, a few thousand feet apart.

I reckon that things had been going along too smoothly for a while, for, as we went to cross defiant Mutton Creek, rumbling and frothing in its impatient rush to the sea, and I tossed the rope over to Bugs to "tow" Red across, Red momentarily panicked and reared back, and came within inches of dragging Bugs into the icy water. But I managed to jump back and whop Red on the rump; and with a mighty leap, he jumped clear across the creek, two hundred pound. pack and all. I held my breath, and I think my heart stopped beating too, as I could just see the pack flying off, and the stampeding horse scattering food, clothing, and shelter down a mile of mountain trail. I was so engrossed with the possible tragedy that I didn't even notice Bugs, who doesn't know yet how he escaped being trampled under thirteen hundred pounds of horse and pack. Red, after the jump, calmly showed his ignorance of anything at all out of the ordinary, completed the jump, and took a few steps and started munching grass. The pack showed not the slightest dislocation. We, however, learned a mighty important lesson. Be always ready for the unexpected, but especially while crossing the treacherous streams.

3:30 PM. We crossed Lewis River; and one hundred yards up the trail we came into Divide Meadow. It was as beautiful as its name, with much grass, ample wood, a fine camp site, and such swarms of mosquitoes as to be unimaginable, except to those who have experienced an encounter with them. Bugs remarked, as he was smashing them with a cup, forty or fifty at a time, on his leg, "I haven't calculated how long it would take, but I believe that if I kept this up long enough, I'd kill every mosquito on Mt. Adams." He gave up, when someone reminded him that they were still multiplying faster than we all were killing them.

The mosquitoes were so bad we unloaded the horses, and Judy and Bugs rode on ahead, looking for a less mosquito infested camp site. The rest of us built a smudge fire as a measure of defense against the poisonous swarms. It helped a little, but they were still the hungriest, smoke eatin'est "skeeters" that ever grew; and we wondered if we tasted as good as smoked ham or sausage.

In about thirty minutes, Judy and Bugs rode back in with good news. In five minutes, we were reloaded and moving on; and by 5:00 we dropped down into a little, grassy vale alongside roaring Adams Creek, and proceeded to make camp. Still, just before this, we had to stop, in spite of the mosquitoes, in a rangy, flower filled meadow, and take a color picture of the horses and some of the party, with massive, Adams Glacier in the background.

By now we were all feeling heavily, the strain of weariness and tension; and as packs were unloaded, I suddenly felt sick to my stomach. It was either the altitude, or the sardines we'd had for lunch; but just as I stretched out on the ground, a cream colored, Piper Clipper came buzzing over. I recognized the airplane as belonging to my friend, Bob Edling, from Dallesport. I leaped up, clawing for my signal mirror, and ran for the nearest patch of sun. But before I could get the mirror into action, he was gone, and evidently had not seen us. Keen disappointment gripped us all, for it seemed incredible that he could find us, down in that tiny defile beneath the trees; but, sure that he would make a second pass, we waited in the fading patch of sun.

Patience rewarded us, for soon he reappeared farther up the Mountain. One flash from the mirror, and he peeled off our way for a beautiful buzz job. Thinking that was all, we waved goodbye, as he disappeared over a ridge. But hardly a moment later he again reappeared at the head of our canyon, and came down just above the trees at half throttle. As he flashed over the camp, a package dropped with a brilliant streamer attached, and landed right next to a very startled Denny, who, as usual, was playing in the water, and hadn't even heard the plane for the roar of the stream. We hastily opened it up, and out tumbled, that morning's Oregonian, a razor and blades, a can of Dr. Scholl's Foot Powder, a recipe for sourdough, a list of ground to air signals, and a note which read, "Hi you all. Hope trip is going well. If there is anything you need, try to spell it out, that is, anything the emergency signals won't cover. I will try to find you again Thursday or Friday. The razor is for Dean. He probably needs a shave by now, doesn't he, Alma? Figured you may like to cook up a batch of meatballs. Nothing exciting going on here. Fair weather, with afternoon thunder east of Cascades is forecast. Good luck to all you lucky people."

With shouts we grabbed four brightly colored air mattresses and laid out two L's on the ground. "All's Well." Another pass over us, and a second package crashed through the trees, and out tumbled three pounds of fresh hamburger. A third pass sent a package down squarely in camp, and revealed a bag marked, "Horse Feed." Oats, flavored with molasses. A fourth streamer came drifting down with a clothespin holding a note, and it lodged thirty feet up in a tree, matted with branches. While Bob patiently circled overhead, Rodney, puffing and blowing in the thin air, managed to struggle up to it and toss it down. It read in part, "How come you didn't stay at old cabin at Divide Meadow? Too many skeeters?... I got your signal, 'All's Well.' See you all in a couple days or so."

We quickly changed the mattresses to a Y, "Yes." A third note landed squarely in camp. "OK, I'll go away and quit spoiling your solitude." We bowed deeply a hearty thanks, and with a wide open pass down through the trees, he left us, and we were suddenly one hundred years back in time.

But excitement still ruled our spirits, and sick stomach, aching feet and shoulders, weariness, and tension just did not exist. It did bother our ego a little that Bob had guessed that the mosquitoes had driven us on; but the new life he had given us sent everyone into the lively spirit of making camp. The living picture, created by some of the kids sitting around blowing up brilliantly colored air mattresses, the horses grazing in the sparse grass at either end of the camp, little Itch helping the boys drag in wood for the fire, and Bugs and I staking the tents while Lorraine and Alma finished preparing our supper, was a living picture indeed.

The women, having no table for their stove, had to get down on their knees to cook. And the other two dogs, sitting behind them, expectantly waiting, was always good for a laugh, or a grin.

During the excitement of the "Air Drop," the women had left their "kitchen" and food completely unattended. They came back down from the clouds with a start to find three, hungry dogs, uninterested in the airplane, testing the partially opened cans of beef stew as if wondering if they dared to steal the "abandoned" food.

After a fine supper of that beef stew with fresh dumplings, Bugs, Bobbie and I bent over two saplings, and tied the food bags on, and released them. The food was now fifteen feet off the ground, away from prowling bears. We finished a wonderful day, sitting around the camp fire, recounting the day's happenings, and watching Alma again sew up Judy's shoe with more fish line.

The author cooling off with Alma and Rainy

Cheechahko's Dream

You can dream of Alaska's mountains,
and a lake that is icy blue,
and a cabin warm where a northern storm
is a symphony just for you.

You can dream of the call of a waterfall
on a tumbling glacier stream,
and picture there a meadow fair
in your "Cheechahko's Dream."

But you'll not be wrong, you tender foot.
Your dream is a vision true;
for Alaska's call is her mountains tall
and her lakes and her glaciers too.

And that silence deep is designed for sleep;
and that cabin's just waiting to grow;
for the timbered land and an eager hand
are the team that can make it so.

So trade your ease for the tundra trees;
leave the world of confusion and strife.
Lift up your eyes to the northern skies,
and discover the secret of life.

June 12, 1961
(From the book, ISLANDS OF EXPERIENCE, by the same author)

This vision appeared first in my wife's mind, then on canvas in oils, and only finally on paper in words. It is a lovely thing, isn't it?

Chapter IV

Lost In A Paradise

Wednesday, August 8th, 1956. 5:30 AM. Our bargain air mattresses were a waste of money, even if they had a big name label. I've patched mattresses every evening, and slept on hard ground three nights in a row. I'm sure that the rest are getting a better average than that. Ah, but we still would not trade this experience for a thousand dollars a day.

The sun came up in the north this morning, or so it seemed, and the air was damp, and colder. We had wonderful, fresh hamburgers for breakfast, thanks to Bob Edging's "Air Drop," but we tried to rush things along so we could get moving before the mosquitoes got too bad, and the creek too high. This creek, like several others, was fed directly from a glacier, and would sometimes double or triple in size as the day warmed up.

9:30 AM. Loaded and underway. The horses crossed the creek very well, considering that it was the noisiest and wildest so far, and, had a very rocky bottom.

But once across, we had to wait on the women and girls, who made, we men thought, a silly detour several hundred yards up the creek where they crawled across on a log on their hands and knees. They didn't appreciate our voicing our disgust. But to be fair, I must admit that part of Alma's difficulty in crossing streams was her justified and wise reluctance to do any jumping that might reinjure her back. This would be no time to lose the ability to walk. Although with the horses we were partially prepared for such an emergency, it would still have been a serious problem.

After a hard, thirty minute climb, we started breaking out of the heavy timber into meadow after meadow filled with masses of flowers. Surely here was all the beauty of famed Bird Creek Meadows. Several varieties of Indian Paint Brush, and a sweet smelling, Lupine like flowers predominated; but there were many, many others as well. Surely, here is proof that the Almighty One creates beauty for the sheer joy of creating beauty. For had no one arrived to drink of this gift, the beauty would have been just as beautiful

Mt. Rainier came clear into our view, and the precipitous, northwest corner of Mt. Adams towered almost overhead. One time, the train moved ahead out of my sight and hearing, while I stopped to make notes. And as I walked on alone, through flowers, flowers, flowers, I poignantly experienced, through the awesome, impressive stillness of the mountains, the gently sad, yet sweet and peaceful loneliness of the wilderness.

10:45 AM. A real view point, and we stopped to thrill at Goat Rocks, Mt. Rainier, and the Cispus River Gorge. For the preceding hour we had been passing pool after pool of crystal clear water, any one of which could be called "Mirror Lake."

11:15 AM. Beautiful, sand bottomed Killen Creek.

12:15 PM. We decided that everyone must be seasoning to the trail. There are less complaints of aches, and pains, and weariness. Of course, the spectacular view after view had really robbed us of any reason to complain. We stopped for lunch, looking north toward Goat Rocks, Mid-way Guard Station, Two Lakes, and Mt. Rainier.

1:15 PM. We loaded up the horses, and set out again upon this wilderness trail. And ten minutes later, we came to a trail junction, but there were no signs which read "Round The Mountain Trail." We were certain that the trail to the right was the one, but the hand printed sign, found lying on the ground, read, "Highline Trail." Although it sounded exciting, and the kids "just knew" it was the correct one, we realized the possibility of finding ourselves deadended up on the side of the Mountain. And with our rations limited to only one extra day's *supply,* we knew that, if we used that extra day wandering around on a false lead, we would have to, purely for safety, take our back trail, and admit that the Mountain had won, this time. However, after Bugs had dropped his pack and scouted ahead on the Crest Trail for half an hour, we decided to chance the Highline trail, and at 2:00 PM, we moved out.

2:30 PM. It was a little warm, and dry, climbing toward the Mountain, so we stopped at the first water for quite a spell. A wee, wee spring, but oh, so good.

2:45 PM. We arrived at the meadow of meadows. The horses were getting hungrier, or the grass was getting tastier. There were numerous, slow moving, small, clear streams threading through, watering the grass; and there were large beds of white flowers whose blossoms were like tufts of silky cotton. Lava Glacier towered fiercely over the south end of the meadow; and huge, white, cumulus clouds towered threateningly, but beautifully, to the north. Hoping to at least reach Red Butte by 4:30, we pushed on through. But the trail so faded out at the head of the meadow by 3:30, that we unloaded the horses packs, and prepared to make camp, while Judy and Bugs rode out to scout the trail.

While they were gone, we moved all the gear out onto a level, grassy, dry glade in the middle of the meadow, gathered wood, and built a fire. Whether we were on the right trail or not, we weren't about to leave this paradise this day.

The air was so still, and the sun so warm, and the little, ribbon like streams so inviting, we decided we should all take baths. So the women and girls went down the meadow, and the boys and I went up. Some of the boys walked over under a water fall and took a shower; but Lloyd and I were chicken, so we stayed down where the water was warmer - like thirty-two and one half degrees, instead of thirty-two.

Just as we finished, and Bobbie was taking a picture of "Lloyd's Dad" standing in the creek with just a thin towel for protection, (We needed proof that we had taken a bath in that icy water.)Judy and Bugs came riding back. My Daughter, having no respect for her Father's modesty, purposely tried to ride right over me in hopes of dislodging the towel. I finally had to pull my rank, and order her back to camp.

They had found no trail. So after a short rest, we saddled up Red again, and I rode, and Bugs walked, so he could scout where the horse couldn't go; and we went back for a more thorough search. In the meantime, the women had cheerfully named our camp, "Lost Camp."

5:30 PM. We were nearly up on the Mountain proper, but still no trail, or way for the horses across the horrible, rocky wash to
the plainly visible, red colored butte that we presumed to be the Red Butte shown on our map. So we split up, and Bugs hiked over toward the butte, and I rode on south, up the side of the Mountain, hoping to find a way to head the mile across wash. In walking alongside Red up one of the many, long, smooth snowfields that would have been a skiers heaven, I was jolted to a stop by the sight of a small child's, fresh, bare, foot prints in the snow. Closer examination showed the toes spread slightly more than normal, and reason demanded that they must be an animal's, probably a bear cub's. However, the sight haunted me for some time, and I expected at moments to hear a child crying.

By 6:00 PM, I had reached a point where I thought a crossing could be made, although it surely would be rough going, so, afraid that the women would be worrying, I rode on back to camp.

7:30 PM. After a wonderful supper of mashed potatoes, and chicken and dumplings, here, on this wild, northern side of this Mountain, I was about to saddle up Red again, and go look for Bugs, when he came steaming in. I don't believe that man ever gets tired. He had been clear over to

Red Butte, had seen a huge buck with branched antlers on one side only, and had found signs of the "trail" back, but no sign of a trail on beyond. We had a job facing us for the next day.

For all of the trail problems, however, we believed that this was the finest camp yet, and if we had all the holes in the air mattresses patched, we were ready for a good night's sleep. We later decided that some of the larger mosquitoes at Divide Meadow had mistaken the mattresses for us, and had drilled too many holes in them to patch.

As we sat around the fire, absorbing its relaxing and healing, spiritual as well as physical warmth, nine year old Denny popped out with a perfect imitation of the radio ad, "My stars, how does Mars make such wonderful candy bars?" Of course we all laughed hilariously, that is, all except Bugs, who didn't think that his youngest should be showing off so. But Denny had warmed to our responses and proceeded to thoroughly entertain us for half an hour with an impromptu production of ludicrous rhymes. His Father acceded to being overruled by the group, and just sat quietly with his head down in amused embarrassment.

But while this "evening's entertainment" was going on, I noticed that Alma, Lorraine, and Bugs weren't drinking their usual evening coffee. When I asked them about it, they all candidly admitted that they were afraid to get up in the middle of the night, and with all the coffee they had been drinking, it was too miserable not to. I thought that was a fine idea, because, the night before, after we had all settled down, and I was just beginning to feel warm and cozy, Judy and Alma insisted that they had to get up, and, I had to go with them, because they were scared. I grumbled as loudly and firmly as I could, at having to crawl out of that nice, warm bed, crawl through the end of the tent, and walk out on the cold ground in my bare feet. But for some reason, they just thought it was funny.

9:00 PM. With a log fire roaring, seven kids giggling with excitement in their sleeping bags, and a million, glittering stars, sending their brilliant, inspiring points into our hearts, we reluctantly went to bed.

The End?

Ah, so 'tis happiness you seek, my friend;
is that your goal?
Take care, lest on its placid sea
you strike a shoal
that pinions you and holds you fast,
so that for you there is not future,
only past.

And all the stormy seas that make a man
must crash and roar against some distant shore
where spirits, charged with battle for this life,
see in the storm the chance to say, "I can,
and ask for more."

Ah yes, I sought for happiness, like you;
and I have found it, largely, that is true.
Nor would I change it at this date I guess,
and yet I wonder, could I honestly confess?

Could I speak out in words that do not lie
and say I've missed the opportunity to cry
alone and frightened on that distant shore
where all my passions from my pen could pour
ten thousand words all whetted to an edge
that cut away the numbing fat of peace
and split the soul from bondage with their wedge?

The Lord of Heaven said, "You seek, you find,"
but here, you see, the problem is the kind
of seeking that obsesses one.
For lest you dare, and I mean dare, my friend,
then happiness could truly be
your end.

June 17, 1964
(From the book, ISLANDS OF EXPERIENCE, by the same author)

Chapter V

The Point Of No Return

Thursday, August 9th, 1956. 6:30 AM. And I was out of bed and starting a fire from last night's coals, and restaking the horses. The sun appeared to be coming square out of the north. It was hard to believe that we were that far around the Mountain.

Bugs, still unsatisfied with what he had found in the way of a trail the night before, and uncertain as to just how he was going to lead us out into the vastness of that rock wash, did some more scouting. He finally found that we had missed a turn in the Highline Trail, and had fortunately come upon this primeval paradise, purely by accident.

9:40 AM. "Tally Ho, let's go." Knowing that we had a lot of rocky ground to go over, we lightened the loads on the horses to save their feet as much as possible. This of course meant an extra ten pounds or so on most of us, but no one complained. We appreciated the horses too much.

We said goodbye to "Lost Camp," better named "Paradise Valley," then up, up, up, straight toward the Mountain. Terrific upheavals of rock were everywhere, and we climbed the snow fields every chance we had. The trail was very difficult to follow, or was even non-existent most of the time, and Red Butte frowned disapproval of our daring. Some of the kids were wishing that they had not lost their colored glasses.

10:20 AM. We found the first real, trail marker, a high pile of rocks; and we crossed treacherous Muddy Fork. As we stopped to reload a camera, someone noted Denny Hill's weight, fifty-two pounds, against his pack, ten pounds; and we discovered that in ratio, he was the heaviest loaded in the party, including the horses. He surely was his Father's Son.

Still we climbed straight toward the Mountain till it seemed we should be able to reach out and touch her. As we stopped once to let the women catch up, I was puzzled to see Lloyd carrying the big coffee pot that was normally in the top of Alma's pack. The (to me) ridiculous truth soon became apparent, as Alma came along with the coffee pot replaced in her pack by a very snooty looking pooch. Itch's feet were sore from running over that volcanic rock, and Mommie felt sorry for her. Itch was even so sure of her position, (socially), that she even growled quite seriously when anyone came near, warning them not to take her out. Alma just grinned, and found herself carrying her much farther than she had intended. Of all the places to baby a useless, if so lovable an animal.

11:00 AM. No trail again. While Bugs scouted ahead for the trail, a Cessna 182 passed close overhead. We flashed the signal mirror; but they failed to see us, or just ignored us.

Bugs found the trail, finally, swinging toward Red Butte, which made us then quite certain that we were on the right trail.

In half an hour we left the wash, but headed into the wildest, jaggedest, lava bed we had ever seen. Amazingly, the trail was better here, and at noon we stopped for family pictures with the back trail for a background. It seemed incredible that we had traversed that horrible wasteland.

There were many large boulders there, with flat surfaces, and the kids found small, chalklike stones with which they had great fun, running ahead and writing signs on the boulders like, "Buy your foot powder here," and, "Do you have that 'Tired feeling?'" The only one that drew any real recognition from Bugs was, "Shop and Save at Hill's Red and White."

12:10 PM. Denny spotted an elk, but they were apparently as flighty as the deer, as it vanished before we all could see it. At the same time we saw an eagle diving at something on the ground; and all of a sudden, we realized that it was little Itch, who had ranged too far ahead. I don't know if the eagle could have carried her off, but there was no question about his trying. We defended our little, problem pet by firing several times at the huge bird; and the kids strained their lungs, in that thin air, calling her back. A few moments later, she came scampering back to us, not the least bit ashamed of the anxiety she had caused.

12:30 PM. The trail vanished again, so we stopped for lunch, with no water, at the highest point on our trek, (we thought,) level with the top of Red Butte, seven thousand, two hundred feet. Pictures, pictures, and we were running out of film. As we ate our lunch, we suddenly realized, with a tremulous thrill, that we were at the "Point of no return" - three and a half days back, three days ahead, three days' supply of food.

Bugs, as was becoming usual, had found the trail, so just before 2:00, with a different brand of sardines under our belts, for variety, we loaded up, and started to climb again, this time, straight toward the east edge of the Mountain. Distances between stops were shorter, our wind was shorter, and tempers were shorter; although good spirits still held. How could it be otherwise with such wild, wild beauty as this?

2:15 PM. The shout went up the line to stop. We heard the Mountain groan. We scanned the precipitous walls, hoping to see an avalanche, but were greeted, only by its massive stillness. Remembering stories of avalanches being started by a rifle shot, we fired several rounds from our pistols at the icy cliffs, but the Mountain didn't even bother to laugh at us. Ten minutes later, we topped the ridge, and left the northern view of Mt. Rainier behind, and looked out, instead, across the Indian Reservation to Yakima Valley. We estimated that we had climbed another several hundred feet since our lunchtime, or to a true high point of nearly eight thousand feet.

We stopped again for a well earned *rest,* and to appreciate the unique position of our view point. The weather was perfect, and up in that high, thin, clear and untainted air, distances were deceiving, so that even far away objects seemed within easy traveling distance. We had to point out landmarks to one another, and give the approximate distance in miles to realize fully the remoteness of our position. In another ten minutes, as we traveled on, Mt. Adams Lake, and Goat Butte, our destination for the day, came into view. And we came to a very steep snow field, about one hundred yards across, on which the kids had a grand time skiing down on their shoes, while Bugs and I precariously zigzagged the horses. And then, for the next half hour, the terrain dropped away so swiftly that the trail repeatedly zigzagged; and we were continually warning the kids to be careful not to roll rocks on others. The horses surprised as well as frightened us often with their mountain goat agility in jumping from point to point, and often stepping around a sharp turn with four feet on four different levels at one time.

3:20 PM. We were down into meadowland again, with water and grass, but the trail yet again faded out. Good old "energy plus" Bugs dropped his pack and ranged ahead, looking for the trail. But after an hour, we gave up, and decided to make camp for the night, right where we were.

After dropping our packs and giving the kids orders on making camp, Bugs and I rode on, looking for the trail. We headed generally for Goat Butte and after a battle with the horses in getting them across the first, turbulent creek, we still found no trail. But we did find very good going until about 5:00 PM, when we came into the small, grassy valley where we thought we had seen a beaten trail from our camp site. It turned out to be a sand wash, but the area was quiet and beautiful, and soon we found a fine camp site, in a small grove of trees. Although there were no mosquitoes, there was a cold wind up on the bench where we had left the party making camp. Still, there was no trail, so, since the vale led to the right of our route to Goat Butte, we decided to climb the ridge ahead and look over.

After a twenty minute struggle up a steep, rock and sandy slope, and through thick, brushy trees, we broke out on the bench of Goat Butte. The thrill of the explorer came over us as we rode across that wild, red, cindery and untouched waste to where we could see down into the Big Muddy, across to the Ridge of Wonders, out to Mt. Hood, and down into the Glenwood Valley. Civilization so near, and yet so far.

We found the trail that led down from the abandoned, Goat Butte Lookout, and, hoping that it would lead us to our "round the mountain trail," we followed it down. But it hadn't been used for so long it soon faded out. The sun was gone behind the Mountain, and with still an hour ride back to camp, we hit our back trail. While we were looking down, over fifteen hundred feet, into the north forks of the Big Muddy, we saw a towering, sandstone wall that would stop further travel that way; so we decided the trail, the trail we were seeking, must head on up the vale in which we had found the camp site.

7:00 PM. We rode into camp, tired, hungry and a little disappointed. Had there been any trail markers at all, as the Forest Service had promised, we could have been settled in the quiet, warm vale camp by 4:00 PM, instead of up on this cold, windy bench. But it was too late to move on, so we staked out the horses and dove ravenously into a fine supper of corned beef hash, hot chocolate, cookies, and pudding, there, on that unknown, wilderness shelf, on the side of the great Mountain. Three times, in the last three hours, we heard. the Mountain speak; only these times we could see the tons of snow crashing down and sending up their clouds of white cold.

All the way over to Goat Butte we had ridden over so many elk tracks, as fresh as our horses foot prints, that we could almost imagine that we were driving a herd of cattle. But we never once saw a live animal.

8:30 PM. The camp fire was burning low, and although spirits were again high, we decided to get the troupe to bed, until suddenly someone discovered a strange, flashing light far off across the reservation. It had a red tinge, and flashed in groups of five, ten, four, and ten again. We watched with puzzled curiosity for half an hour; but the mystery remained a mystery, so we all went to bed.

The wind was up some more, and was probing the openings in our clothing; but the sky was still ablaze with stars; and in that thin, clear air, the milky way painted a white path from north to south. We gazed with some awe for yet a little while, for never before had we seen the heavens so magnificently declaring the Glory of God.

The Glacier Priest

Across the frigid water stands
the lonely Glacier Priest;
his sermon never ending as
you stand alone and feast
your eyes upon this monument
of God's creation plan
of tall, eternal mountain that
is part of mortal man.

Your ears may strain to listen
to the voice of which I speak
and hear no sound
but the wind around
each tall and lonely peak.
So listen with your eyes my friend,
and think on Him above;
and let the mountain tell your heart
of the vastness of His love.

Climb slowly with your eyes my friend
up ragged center ridge,
and note the care
that was taken there
to carve each stony bridge,
as if in all creation He
had nothing more to do
than to carve this craggy mountain and
create the one called you.

For such is truth,
like eternal mountain,
standing tall and strong:
you were prepared
with far more care
than was this misty song.

So remember, when you leave this place
and reach another shore,
that life is not just food and fun;
this mountain says there's more;
And remember too this Glacier Priest,
when you have gone beyond,
will still be standing there
and preaching
across this arctic pond.

February 23, 1961
(From the book, ISLANDS OF EXPERIENCE, by the same author)

Chapter VI

We "Cross Over The Bridge"

Friday, August 10th, 1956. 6:00 AM. The sun was shining through the walls of our mountain tents. I stepped out into still, warm, clear, and oh so clean and fresh, morning air. Adjectives sound trite, and words fail, as I try to describe the view of the Mountain. For sheer cliffs, color, castle like promontories of rock, and gleaming, glacier filled gorges, this picture, with the bright, morning sun at our backs, topped them all. This morning, more than any other, the gentle, yet powerful "presence" of the Mountain filled our souls.

The horses nickered, and tossed their heads impatiently. They had learned that almost the first thing I did was to re -stake them out for a tasty breakfast of mountain greens.

Even a short hike up away from camp became an experience unforgettable. Seating myself on a large, pink and purple boulder, with the Mountain impressing its presence over my shoulder, I looked off north, and saw the jagged teeth of Goat Rocks, and just below them, low clouds forming a river of billowy cotton flowing down into the upper reaches of the Klickitat.

7:00 AM. We checked the horses feet. Their shoes showed the wear of miles of grinding, volcanic rock, but their feet were in remarkably good condition.

Breakfast: "I can smell the bacon frying, hear it sizzling in the pan, hear the breakfast horn in the early morn, drinkin' coffee from a can." Oh, if only a man could make a living at a life like this.

As we lined up for breakfast, our scout returned from following a hunch and reported finding the trail well above us. We had missed it where it was hidden under a large snowfield. Bugs had been clear over behind Goat Butte, and said that we could have been there in another hour last night, but again, we believed that our tough luck was our good fortune. This way, we had this marvelous view, with the sun just right for pictures, and we had a thrilling part of the trail yet ahead.

9:40 AM. With a long trail ahead of us, and our fine trail scout in the lead, we left "Ghost Camp" behind. The strange, flashing light, and the cold, eerie wind, and the Mountain's groanings, last night, had given the camp its name. In a few minutes, we had the horses and Denny across the creek without too much difficulty, and were one hundred yards up the line, only to find the women and the rest of the kids and three dogs, Jinks, Margy, and Itch, were not with us. Bugs and I hiked back, and there they were, half way to Mt. Adams, it seemed, trying to find a way across. And they had been doing so well.

10:25 AM. Bugs led us back onto the main trail. The frequent scarcity or non-existence of trail markings led someone to make the amusing observation that the old, horse manure we found along the way made better trail markings than those provided by the U.S. Forest Service. Another ten minutes, and we headed the draw that ran up from the vale camp we had found last night, and topped the divide between the headwaters of Muddy Fork of the Cispus, and Rusk Creek, a north fork of the Big Muddy. The waters were running southeast now.

A short way down the trail, we came to a tiny lake, on the edge of a bench - and lost the trail again. Although our film was really running low, we couldn't resist another

picture of the horses and lake, with those terrible, towering reaches of rock and ice for a background. Our wonderful women were out with Bugs, scouting for the trail. Somehow, I found my pencil saving me much extra hiking, but the good sports never complained.

11:10 AM. They found the trail again.

11:30 AM. We came into full view of the sandstone wall which, with its vari-shaded hues of orange and gold, shaded into rust and pink, and sharply silhouetted against a clear, blue sky, looked like a misplaced part of Arizona, here, in this volcanic region; and we stopped to stare in wonder at the awful sculptury of wind and weather. If Yosemite, The Grand Tetons, or the Colorado had no more than duplications of what we were seeing this day, they would be wonderlands indeed.

As we walked on the slope under the wall, we noticed trees that had been knocked down, or sheered off. And there were immense boulders, weighing several tons, resting here and there. They had tumbled down from that wall, some, not too long before. We joked, but not without some seriousness too, that we'd best keep the two pack horses well apart for the thousand feet or so of danger area. If a boulder came down, and wiped out one horse and pack, the surviving members of the party would still have one horse and pack left. For all of its beauty, we breathed easier when we were clear of that silent, fascinating tower of poised devastation. As we dropped on down the side of Cunningham Ridge, the trees began to thicken, and the roar of the Big Muddy became louder.

12:00 Noon. We lost the trail again, and the trustworthy scouts ranged out. But those of us with the horses didn't mind. We fully used the time drinking deeply of our last view of the wonders that were ours.

Fifteen minutes later, the trail again, and this time a well beaten one on an easy incline, and we really made good time. So we hiked on till nearly 1:00 PM, when we stopped for lunch in the welcome shade of a thick grove of trees. We had left the outstandingly spectacular behind, and had, largely, just miles ahead. But legs and shoulders were toned and seasoned to the trail now, and anyway, we could live for days on the memories of the things we had seen and done.

1:30 PM. Only a half hour break, but all were eager to go, so we quickly loaded up and moved off down the trail; down, down, down. A look up through the trees showed clouds forming around the Mountain for the first time since we left our cars and their symbols of civilization. Could it be that the Old Man was sad that we were leaving? We are in bear country again. We see tree after tree torn by their claws; and some marks were very fresh.

2:00 PM. Pine and Fir trees, and Laurel, and, the Mulligan Butte Trail junction. Down, down, down. No one wanted to stop, even for a break, except once, when Lorraine, struggling with her pack over a fallen tree, lost her balance and landed on her back in a tangle among the branches. Thinking, from her moans, that she was seriously hurt, we rushed over to help. But we found only that the weight of her pack, her weariness, and the tangle of branches, had her completely helpless. Bugs quickly grasped the opportunity to take a revealing picture.

Not counting blisters, Lorraine's fall proved the only casualty of the entire adventure, although it was not discovered until two months later when she went to the Doctor with a sore rib. X-rays showed that she had broken the rib in the fall. But at the time, we were brought out of our laughter to the seriousness of keeping constant watch on the horses. Someone looked up to see Benny down on his knees, and all ready to roll - with the full pack on his back.

3:00 PM. We found fresh, caulked shoe marks in the trail, and ten minutes later, fresh jeep tracks, not over an hour old. We wondered if someone had been up looking for us. And there were names and dates carved into the bark of the Birch trees. I guess Indian kids are kids too. Down, down, down, and an hour later, the first Oak trees, and some Tamarack; and the Ponderosa Pine trees were becoming true to their species, huge, yellow and beautiful. And the years of accumulation of fallen pine needles made a soft and scented carpet over which we silently trod.

As we stopped to appreciate Jo Ann's discovery of some of the most beautiful, pale blue lilies, with a faint, sweet fragrance, little Itch came running up with a mouth full of Porcupine quills. We had no choice, but to stop the whole train, tie a stick in her mouth, and go to work. We managed to jerk most of them out with our fingers, but we had to file the edges off of Bobby's nail clippers, with my own nail file, to improvise a pair of pliers, to pull the rest. After that half hour struggle, we moved on with, we hoped, a wiser pet.

Only a lovable, little animal such as this curiously named one, could have received such attention, and caused such a disruption, without rupturing the deep affection that all had for her. Although homely, feisty, and remarkably talented, she also had that indescribable power of just walking into people's hearts in a way that said, "Well, I'm here. Love me." And we did. I reckon that the only true measure of love is the depth of sorrow felt when such loved ones, whether human, or animal, are taken away. And truly that measure was felt to the full when, a few months later, this "pint-sized" but vital part of our family failed to rally from an attack of distemper. We shall miss her; we shall deeply miss her.

5:15 PM. Daylight was rapidly fading, and though the foliage, Vine Maple, White Fir, and Ferns among the Pines, told us that we were down to the elevation of Glenwood Valley, we still had found no "Yakima Highway," the lightly used, dirt road into the Reservation from Glenwood, for which the bridge we were seeking was built. With less than two hours of daylight remaining, and at least an hour required for setting up camp, and with our map showing nearly an hour's travel to Cougar Guard Station, after we crossed the bridge, we were becoming concerned with the narrowing margin of time. There would be weary bones, and aching feet before this day ended.

5:25 PM. We had found the highway; and as we walked the road southward, we soon heard the rushing, roaring waters of the Big Muddy again. And shortly after, as we crossed the bridge over the deep, steep walled chasm, we had to repress a surge of emotion as we realized the victory over that turbulent, brown torrent that had defied us for the last, eight, weary hours. Hold up a little longer, aching feet, and we can rest for the night.

6:15 PM. A '56 Hudson came from behind, and an Indian couple stopped. We asked him how much farther to the Cougar Guard Station. He pointed and said, "Right there." And a few more steps ahead brought the cabin into view.

There was no one there to whom we could show that precious, little pink slip that we had worked so hard to get, so we packed up behind the cabin a hundred yards or so, and started making camp in a park like area beneath the huge Yellow Pines. The girls all headed for Cougar Creek to take a bath, while we made camp; then our turn came, while they cooked a hungrily accepted supper of beans, ryetack, and chocolate pudding. We never thought we'd so enjoy a bath in ice water, but the last several miles were the dustiest of the whole trip; and with the day being the longest, this bath became an emotional as well as a physical transformation.

As we ate, there by the fire, in the darkening night, we debated the next day's route. Although we were all weary from a long, hard day, we still wanted to try to make it home by Saturday night or early Sunday morning, so, since the trails and markers had been so poor, we decided to try the short cut, via Shadow Lake, and the logging roads, that I had discovered from the air.

This night, there was little lingering around the camp fire. We felt only the intense desire to crawl into bed, somewhere, anywhere, and go to sleep. But even as we did so, we laughed at one another as we groaned over our protesting joints and muscles, and compared the sizes of blisters on our feet.

It was not until some weeks later, as we were reminiscing together, that we even thought of the incongruity of our meeting with the Indian couple. Eleven "pale faces," walking a dusty trail, and leading two pack horses, were met by an Indian couple in a modern car. I wonder yet, if they too smiled at that incongruity. Things have changed, in a hundred years.

The Highline Trail

Nature's Song

A glacier glows mid mountains tall and cold.
Like the stream that drifts away it's ages old.
Yet year by year the mountain snows press down
to form anew this frozen, jeweled crown.

And out across the tundra from its base
a trapper's cabin nestles in the lace
of trees that formed of water glacier fed,
and soil ground from rocks that were its bed.

Time is a word, but what is time?
The cabin's old; the trees have stood so long.
Yet in the measure of the river and her crown,
they're both but one refrain from nature's song.

June 13, 1961
(From the book, ISLANDS OF EXPERIENCE, by the same author)

Chapter VII

How Much Farther, Daddy?

Saturday, August llth, 1956. 5:30 AM. I couldn't stay in bed any longer, so got up and built a fire, restaked the horses, and then stepped down to that rushing creek for a refreshing wash. It was so interesting to note the things we could do, and enjoy, when we had to. The meals, simple and plain by necessity, tasted better than dinner at the Bohemian, the evening fire was enjoyed more than the finest central heating, and we slept sounder than we would have on the wonderful beds of the North Bend Hotel.

6:30 AM. The rest started crawling out, and we heard the familiar whistle of air coming out of the mattress valves. The Pine Squirrels chattered an unwelcome good morning; and they even tried to insult us by not too inaccurate bombing with pine cones.

Bobbie started the morning laughter with his account of being awakened in the middle of the night with a huge, dark form standing over him, and breathing in his face. He nearly suffocated, down inside his sleeping bag, before he decided he had to have air. As he cautiously peeked out, he saw that it was only Benny, who had gotten loose and was innocently searching for sugar cubes.

9:30 AM. After another fine breakfast of hotcakes, ham and hot chocolate, we left warm and beautiful Cougar Camp, and started down the road. Judy, Lorraine, and Alma, were threatening, by now, to pull my whiskers out, one by one. I think they would have appreciated my "beautiful" beard, if Bugs hadn't deserted me, and shaved nearly every day. As we stopped, once more, to retape Judy's ailing shoe with the last of the tape, we noted down that, next time, we must bring, not only more rolls of tape, but more rolls of film, - oh yes, and more rolls of toilet paper too.

An hour along the road, we left the Yakima Highway, and turned west on a logging road, and started the long, long climb back toward our Mountain. It was typical, Glenwood, summer weather, hot, and sweaty. The logging road ran out in half an hour or so, and we battled over some pretty rough, logged over country until noon, when we broke out onto the good logging road I had been looking for, and we crossed the Hell Roaring Irrigation Ditch. The inspiration of the Mountain was not with us, as we ate our lunch, quiet, hot, tired, and hungry. However, Denny, gulping down his sixth lunch of sardines and ryetack, like the rest of us, provided the laugh of the hour by piping up with a straight face, "I hate this stuff." He never missed a bite.

1:10 PM. We loaded up the horses, and took a long drink. It would be a long way to water. As we sweated and trudged up the dusty logging roads (my shortcut,) I saw that I was swiftly losing popularity. They remembered too well the clean and inspiring, even if sometimes rocky, trails. I knew that I'd better get them to the road to Shadow Lake very soon.

2:20 PM. After struggling out through the raw timber for half an hour or so, even tearing some packs on the horses, on the close packed trees, we struck an old trail that swung in the general direction we wanted to go, so we decided to take it. In about twenty minutes we broke out into open, parklike terrain, and stopped for a "feast" of wild strawberries. In another ten minutes, we found a cold, clear, welcome spring in a grove of Quaking Aspens. Among all the names carved on the trees was, "A. Beeks, 1938." We wondered if it could be my fellow employee, Allen.

About this time, Sherry picked the top off of a wart, and went screaming to her Mother, certain that she was bleeding to death. But she calmed down when her Mother showed her that the biggest part of the hemorrhage was from her handful of crushed strawberries.

3:15 PM. Again, time was slipping away from us, and we still had a long way to go. As we struck out, with no trail, in a west-northwest direction, Bugs and Lorraine suddenly realized, again, that neither had their camera. With a long, look (that had a meaning other than devoted love) at his lovely wife, Bugs dropped his pack and started back to look for the camera. We expected quite a wait, but in little more than ten minutes, here came that tireless man with the camera, shaking his head. This was only one of several times that each had thought the other had the camera, and Bugs had ended up backtracking for it. We could see a slight strain in marital relations developing.

As we battled on, again, through the sometimes thick and brushy timber, everyone was discreetly quiet about their opinions of my "shortcut," but again, Denny's unintended humor came to the rescue. Out of the quiet of a break, he innocently, and candidly said, "I think we should have stuck to the trail."

4:30 PM. After a long and most unpleasant time, struggling uncertainly up through tangles of trees and brush, we found the abandoned road to Shadow Lake. It had grown over so, that it was almost unrecognizable as a road, but its width, and occasional. wheel tracks, impressed in the earth, told us that it had to be the road. By now, however, I felt my popularity was really at a low ebb, and was feeling pretty bad for having led the party into that mess. As can well be understood, I was later very much relieved, when Alma and Lorraine laughingly confessed that the Forest Service had affirmed our suspicions, when the women stopped there on their way home, by admitting that the Forest Service trail, up through the Hell Roaring Gorge, would have been nearly impassable. I think that the women were relieved too.

5:00 PM. The Cattle Drift Fence; and five minutes later, Cress Sheep Camp and wonderful water. We now knew where we were for sure, and could at least relax and just climb, without the strain of wondering. We were still hoping to at least reach Bird Creek Meadows by dark.

5:30 PM. The horses were getting hungry, but so were we; and the kids were asking the repeated question, "How much farther, Daddy?" We sighted our Mountain again, and Bugs cracked a little under the strain. He took off running up the road, and hollering. We finally calmed him down, and then resumed our trudge, trudge, trudge, up, up, up the long road.

Knowing that the next few miles would be plain exertion, we allowed ourselves to slip into a sort of timeless trance. I guess the horses were victims of the hypnosis of unnumbered step, step, step too, for Benny, suddenly coming to his senses, and realizing that Red had slipped ahead out of sight and sound, let out a screeching whinny, right behind Rod, who was leading him. I don't think that you could have shocked that boy more if you had thrown a barrel of ice water on him in the middle of the night. I'll always swear that he jumped clear over two, small Pine trees, and then just folded up in a heap.

At another time, and in much the same way, Alma was brought out from the effects of natures, merciful sedative, by the bellowing and crashing of a three hundred pound calf, headed straight for her, and about ten feet away. She leaped to one side, wondering why at any time, much less this time, she had been chosen as a lady, bull fighter. Her heart didn't stop pounding, but her sense of humor was quickened into laughter, when the calf sidled up to a large, white faced cow a few dozen feet away. The train had silently moved between Mother and baby, and the poor "little" thing was simply rushing home to Mama.

6:20 PM. We came to a view point where we could look down into Bench Lake, and across the wide space to Goat Butte, and the south side of the Ridge of Wonders. It looked like a long, long way. And it had been. We also encountered the first mosquito trouble since entering the Indian Reservation. We decided that the mosquitoes didn't know that they could get a permit for crossing the Indian Lands.

7:00 PM. "The road, the Bird Creek Meadows Road," and our trusty trail scout, Bugs, had been ahead and found a fine, grassy hideaway with a small creek, just off the road. He even had a fire going. No one questioned the idea of no more travel for the day. It was good that this long, weary day had come at this stage of our travels. The tasks of making camp, cooking supper, and caring for the horses, were pretty routine by now, so that, even exhausted as we all were, and with darkness falling swiftly, we were completely settled in a very short time.

Up until this time, I had been having a secret laugh, because my pack was getting lighter, as the stove gas was used up. But as I went to set up the stove for the first time (for me) on the whole trip, I discovered soap, towels, sponges, pieces of cooking equipment, and other odd items, that my "loving" wife had been secretly stashing in around the burners each morning as she folded up the stove. Oh, in mock seriousness, I made my complaints, of course; but such was the wonderful spirit of camaraderie, that we all just laughed with a joyful laughter.

Sweaty and dusty as we all were, we all wanted a bath, but Alma started something by heating water and taking a sponge bath near the fire. We knew, by now, that we had plenty of stove gas for such a luxury. The rest of us quickly followed the example, all, that is except Bugs, whose modesty drove him to somehow manage to bath in the minute confines of his Mountain Tent. Down on his knees, with his head and elbows brushing the top and sides of the tent, and his flashlight silhouetting his every move against the tent walls, he made a far more entertaining show than any of us had around the fire.

But Alma didn't escape being the object of laughter; for once, as she went to cool off her bath water from a bucket that Lloyd had carefully brought her from the creek, she was almost frightened into throwing the water all over the camp. A huge frog left the bucket with a startling splash. The darkness, and the wine of weariness had softened and gentled our spirits. The laughter was a welcome ingredient in the miracle of the healing process.

We were scheduled to be eating this meal at home, so the cooks had to dig into the emergency rations. But by mixing four different soup mixes together, they cooked up a brew that hungry, mountain travelers richly enjoyed. Of course, hungry as we all were, after such a long and arduous day, the powdered potatoes tasted like fresh mashed, and the Spam like beef steak (almost.) But Bugs felt it was a bit of dirty cricket when Alma dug a large can of fruit cocktail out of her food bag for us, and they had none.

9:30 PM. After watching the brilliancy of shooting stars for half an hour, in the high, clear air, even tired as we were, we left the campfire, reluctantly, and went to bed. The quiet of drowsiness was settling over the camp, when sudden laughter broke from Bugs' and Lorraine's tent. The heady wine of our weariness, and our near victory, were still giving us the carefree attitude of the tavern. Like a dutiful, little, wife, Lorraine had reached over to kiss her husband goodnight, and had given the smooth side of his leather jacket, which he was using for a pillow, a resounding smack before realizing her error. Bugs, to our entertainment, didn't take the incident as a compliment.

But only a few moments more, and the weight of that weariness, and the quiet of a cool, mountain night, carried us off into a well earned, carefree oblivion.

Alaska's Mountains

There are mountains high
and mountains low
and mountains round and worn
and mountains hot and mountains cold
and mountains cragged and shorn
of all but frost and
clinging ice
where the williwaw is born.

Oh give me mountains
for my life,
and give me mountains high,
and give me mountains
streaked with snow
where the lonely eagles fly;

Where life is full,
and life is real,
and it's made for you and I;
where freedom swings
on wild wind wings
and I can live
      with the sun
         and the sky.

February 24, 1961
(From the book, ISLANDS OF EXPERIENCE, by the same Author.)

Chapter VIII

The Thrill Of Victory

Sunday, August 12th, 1956. 4:45 AM. Up with the first shift of mosquitoes, I built a roaring fire, and restaked the horses, and then started shouting reveille, and prepared to laugh again at the comedy of watching the women and Bugs come crawling out of the little holes in the ends of the Mountain Tents, blinking their eyes like prairie dogs. This was the last day, and I suddenly realized where Bugs got all that energy I envied so. He was always the last one up; and this morning was even worse. He reminded me of an old engine I once had on a Tugboat. Hardest thing in the world to start, but once started., it was a powerhouse, and was even harder to stop.

We are nearly back to civilization, and I saw my first deer cross the head of the meadow.

5:15 AM. With breakfast cooking, and with supplies running low, I caught Alma thinning the syrup with water again. Bobbie called over from his bed that he had ham and eggs, with toast and jelly ordered, but strangely, the cooks ignored him. "Gotta rustle, everyone. Five miles of trail ahead, and we must get Judy into town in time to swim in the aquacade.

I was amazed. The kids were rolling air out of their mattresses, and rolling up bags without orders. As Bugs knocked down our Mountain Tent, he complained, very loudly, of finding candy wrappers, again, on Alma's side of the tent. We all reminded her that all the food was supposed to be on a share and share alike basis. The pervading spirit of the troupe has changed. There is a spirit of frivolity, almost hilarity, that rules us now.

It has been interesting to note the remarkable improvement in appetites as the days passed by. For the first few mornings, there were hotcakes left over; but this morning, with the same ration, there was never less than two or three in the chow line till the last drop of batter was scraped from the pail.

7:00 AM. An early start, and with the last lap ahead, someone punned, "Well, he who laps last, laps best." It was warm, clear, and beautiful still, and as we climbed again, still closer to "Our Mountain," we felt again the deep, emotion stirring impression of its nearness. Yes, "...give me mountains for my life..."

7:45 AM. Bird Creek Meadows. We stopped for pictures, and registered on a scrap of paper in the empty registry box. As we moved through the meadows, with anxious eyes looking forward, and with the memory of those massive fields of beauty, just over there on the other side of that big, snow covered rock, we paid little attention to the hailed beauty here. No trudging, plodding steps now. Sore feet and aching shoulders, though not forgotten, were ignored, as we stepped along at a fast and happy pace. Even the horses sensed the nearness of the end, and trod close to our heels.

8:40 AM. We sighted Trout Lake Valley, and stopped for a break. Itch and Jinks were chasing each other over the snow fields, but Margy was either being a lady, or showing her age. She was lying down in a pool of melted snow water.

As we traveled on, we were all glad that these final hours found us crossing snow fields, and feeling the fresh breath of the mountain breezes. They re-kindled our enthusiasm for the mountain trails. The dampening effect of the heat and sweat of yesterday was forgotten.

9:10 AM. We topped the ridge. Our last real climb was passed, and we started down to Timberline Camp, and the cars. A Marmot whistled a salute as we filed by.

9:40 AM. "The cars, the cars," and we heard, "Dibbies on the shower first," "When I get home, I'm going to buy the biggest, chocolate malt I can buy," "Boy, me for a juicy hamburger with lots of onions," and, "All I want is to spend the rest of the week in a nice, soft bed."

9:45 AM. We came up to the cars, and felt the thrill of victory, as the full awareness of our achievement swept over us.

> We thrill the thrill of victory,
> beneath the morning sun,
> and praise the Name
> of Him Who knows
> that we have dared, and won.
>
> Yet though we dared, we know full well,
> that never could it be,
> without the Grace
> of Him Who guides
> our daily destiny.

There have been those, and will be those who say ours was a foolish venture. But we who traveled the rugged trail know that our lives will be richer and fuller, because, we dared, and won.

We took our last pictures, and, from habit formed from the last six days, dove into the job of unloading the horses. In minutes we were ready to reload the cars. As I unlocked the car door, a note fell out, which read, "Please appear in Police Court Monday morning for overtime parking fine. Thank you. S.J.B.

We were back to civilization.

From left to right
Bugs, Sherry, Alma, Jo Ann, Lorraine, Judy, Bobbie, Denny, Rod and Lloyd